JAKE CARTWRIGHT

Falling inlove with Sarah

<u>Independent Trucks</u>

I found myself on the greyhound bus. Going back to California. From home, In arizona… I went in search of a close friend of mine. I thought I could possibly find him on the beach where we lived, homeless. I arrived in Los Angeles, Took the metro to Venice Beach and was there for about 3 to 4 days. Only this time, I was lost. Looking around with no friends around. I couldn't stand looking and seeing almost everyone that was homeless high, high out of their minds. Not taking care of themselves… I felt some kind of way. I was upset. This was the day I said no more, hard core stuff. I was on the road to fixing things. So I decided… I leave. Once I figured I wasn't going to find Ray, I decided to go. Where? I wasn't totally sure yet. But before that, James, Tyrell, Ray and I had traveled to Santa Cruz on foot and bus from Venice about a few months before. So then, I said North. Santa Cruz, Mount shasta. Somewhere North. I took my skateboard and started to ride. I rode my skateboard from Santa Monica to North Malibu. I got about a bus or two to take me as far as I could up malibu. Then I started walking. I got about half way before Malibu and Ventura before these two young ladies decided to pick me up. They were driving a red two door volkswagen. I got in the back and they drove me to Northern Oxnard. Gave me a few bucks and I was on my way. I rode my skateboard around oxnard trying to find my way north. I ended up sitting in a Starbucks for a few good hours contemplating my next steps. I was tired of not being healthy and fit. So when I left the Starbucks I found some rocks… and put them in my backpack.. to add weight.. then I started to do pushups at every other bus stop and almost every other light. Until my arms hurt. That day, the sun was almost half way *down and I ran into a young guy around my age and he offered a place for me to stay. His trailer he rented on someone's property. So I stayed, we smoked American spirits and talked about our journeys. I slept well and woke up early and left. The day before I had planned out the locations and easiest way up to Santa cruz from where I was. So I rode my skateboard to this bus stop, this bus wasn't a regular bus though, it was almost like a charter bus that took you from Oxnard to Santa barbara. I got to the bus departure on the end of town. I spanged up some money, $20 dollars exactly to get to Santa Barbara. I got on the bus, and to Santa Barbara I was going.*

BEFORE SARAH..

I got to Santa Barbara… it was late…I rode around. I talked to girls, I sat at the starbucks, I started planning hygiene, a shower, a meal. So I found this place that let you shower, and gave clothes to the young homeless 18-25. I rode there, I got some clean clothes, some shorts, a muscle cut out tee shirt. I'm pretty sure it was a volcom shirt. And some boat shoes… oh and white socks hahaha.. Also I took a shower and got some hygiene stuff, like another toothbrush, some toothpaste.. and not to forget a bunch of lotion. Good smelling lotion. And sunscreen. Then I left and rode around Santa Barbara looking for a place to sleep that night… I found a spot. And got my z's… I woke up the next morning ready to get to the next bus stop. I was there, Doing 20 to 50 pushups at a time. With the backpack with plus rocks and books that I had got from the donation place. It was pretty heavy. I decided to just keep doing calisthenics, Why not. It will keep me in shape and hey I'd probably look good in this muscle shirt. So I got on a bus that morning and it was a long ride. I got dropped off at Santa Maria CA, It was cold, a really small town. But I rode around.. Doing pushups at the bus stop, all over. I was doing squats, jumping jacks. Anything I could. I rode *around looking to get some money to get on the next bus to Santa Luis Obispo. I ran into a young lady, I can't remember her name but we talked and she offered to buy me a jacket and some coffee. We went to a thrift shop I got a jacket and she drove me to the closest starbucks. We drank coffee and talked, I told her what I had been through recently. She offered to take me to burning man with her... I declined nicely.. She went on her way and I stayed at the starbucks. People were coming into the Starbucks at about 10 pm in the morning. When a man came up to me and asked me if I needed anything and he said, can I do anything for you? Can I pray for you? So I talked to him and told him I needed to get to Santa Luis Obispo. He had to problem saying Id love to give you a ride.. We got some more coffee, and started a pretty long drive to Santa Luis Obispo. He prayed for me and I also told him about what I had been going through. He was very cool, good guy. He prayed for on the ride there. We got there later that afternoon. And he had told me safe travels and gave me $50. It was very generous. I went into a local dollar store to buy some snacks and food for the next few days. I came out and went straight to the bus stop... I wasn't sure if it was going to show. I did my pushups and workouts and ended up just hanging out for awhile.. then they bus showed up! And I was heading to Monterey CA. It was late and I ended up sleeping almost all the way. I arrived in Monterey very late. I walked around. It must have been a weekend because there were a lot of people. Enjoying themselves. Drinking, Laughing, Smoking maryjane. I wanted to get some sleep before I got on the next bus to Santa Cruz. So I found a spot. I rolled a fat joint and smoked, then I was snoozing again. All the way through the night in my sleeping bag... I woke up and needed to just relax for the day and not rush to Santa Cruz.. I hung out. Enjoyed the area, I hung with some of the local homeless. I smoked them out with a few joints, here and there. It became night. I found another sleeping spot by the shore. Next to some boats and seals barking all night. Another homeless kid came to the spot I was sleeping at and I decided to share the spot for the night we shared some weed and he lit a tiny tiny, little fire. It was a bit cold. We fell asleep. The next morning, It was chilly and early. I got up and headed to the bus stop. I was on my way to Santa Cruz... I passed Beach City and saw Santa Cruz right in front of me!*

Sometimes Love is short. But this Love is Forever

I got off the bus. The sun was coming out and it was getting warm.. this was my third or fourth time in Santa Cruz. I made my way to the homeless shelter to get food for the day. Then I ate, and signed up for a room. It was a very long wait. I walked to the river and sat on some grass. Enjoyed the weather and said what a city. The beauty was there. I did my workouts and took a nap or two. Then I rode my skateboard *on the strip. All around looking for people to meet and chill with. I did, people were chill. I slept that night on the side of a coffee shop. I woke up and rode to a starbucks instead of blowing my cover at the coffee shop. I sat in front of the starbucks. About 30 minutes went by and this guy came around the corner and asked if I wanted a coffee. I said sure! He came out and sat next to me, we talked. He said he wanted to help me. Asked if I needed anything, if maybe I needed a bigger backpack.. I told him I was going to northern california and he said I would need an actual backpack. So we got in his car and he started explaining how he was a father and felt like if he had a son in my situation he would want someone helping his kids. We drove to a store that sold travel equipment and we looked at backpacks I tried getting the most cheapest one he told me not to. He insisted on buying me a really good one, it was like almost a $100 dollar backpack... Then I bought the backpack and we headed back to the car, I almost broke down.. he said don't feel that way, and offered to get my hair cut. I didn't deny it, I didn't say no. We went to a hairstylist and they cut my hair. I was looking good! We left and kept hanging for the day. He took me to an early lunch and we sat in his car eating sandwiches and talking about how he was leaving back to the Midwest that day. He cried a bit, felt bad. But said safe travels! I am so very blessed for you man! Whoever you are, I still remember that day. You made it easy that day, you made me feel good! You made me feel right! So he dropped me off at the coffee shop that I slept at before and I went to sleep early but people were not around and the coffee shop was closed and the sun was down... I fell asleep... the next morning I woke up and headed to a church that fed the homeless. It was the 117 Chapel, in Santa Cruz. I entered and sat down and listened to the pastor before he fed us. Then we ate! Bread, Cereal, coffee! I hung out and smoked some cigs... and then I headed out those front doors. It was early and crisp in the morning that day.... The sun was bright... so beautiful*

SARAH O'CONOR..
MY LOVE

I walked down the steps with my coffee and took a left to see a big tree and a parking lot across the street... there was this energy. Something I just could not be bothered from, something I was so attracted to... what was it? I crossed the street, to smell some maryjane burning, I looked to the right of me and I seen her. This blonde hair, Blue eye girl. She looked at me and smiled, I was in complete awe. I didn't know what to say, she spoke. "You want to hit this bowl? Want to smoke?" I replied "Sure". I walked up to her then sat down on her right.. I was looking at this girl... like.... I have never seen someone so beautiful. Her skin was glowing against the early sun, her beautiful blue eyes were reflecting in the light... I gazed. "You going to hit this?" I reached for the bowl and started smoking... We started talking. I told her how I was traveling, she said she was heading to work and that was her spot in the morning, Where she smoked mostly. We chatted a bit more, then she said she had to go to work down at the Arcade at the beach. We smiled at each other and then she said, "Well, If you want.. we can smoke later when I get off... Let's meet here?"

I replied "Oh, Yeah. Of course.. lets."

She got up and rode her skateboard off to work... I sat there. Lost for a sec, Wondering what had just happened to me. I had never seen someone like her. I was so, so very happy. I was beyond joyful. I ended up riding around looking for my friend Gabriel. I ran into an older guy named Joseph and he had offered me some Maryjane, he was really cool. Homeless but traveling, he had dread he had red high top converse on. He was like a surfer guy. He had style and his weed was really strong. He tried giving me some papers and they all flew away in the air, but for some reasonI just felt like it was so mystical. I still remember that day.

I found Gabriel and we rode around on our skateboards. Then across from the parking lot where I had met Sarah there was an alley with a tiny parking lot between the alley and the street. Gabriel and I had found a spot to kick it for a while... it started to get later in the day, the sun started going down. We kept burning the herb, and talked. I worked out, we just relaxed. Then out of nowhere, I hear another skateboard. It was her, She rode up and said, "Lets smoke" She had explained it was a long day and she was ready to just chill. I rolled a pretty big hawker and we started burning it down. Gabriel, Me, and Sarah. To be really, really honest, I can't remember a lot of what we talked about right there and then. But she got up after about an hour and said "Well I'm going home now" but then was giving me eye contact and said to me "You coming?"

I looked at Gabriel and told him id see him later... Sarah and I rode our skateboards up the rode out of the strip... We road to her neighborhood. It was a little bit away from where we were but we got there. It was this blue house, We got off our skateboards and walked up to the side of the house. She told me she had roommates and she would introduce them to me later on but we went through the back and went to her room... the lights were low and it was definitely a feeling I had never felt before.. "Take you backpack off, and relax for a bit" I took off my backpack and from behind she put her arms around me, She then turned me around and we started kissing.. it happened quick.. very fast. Then we were laying in her bed and she said "Wine time?" I replied "Lets"... She grabbed a bottle of wine out of her little cooler next to her bed. And she got into some sweats and we went outside to her backyard.. There was a white table and some chairs, We sat down and she started to pour the wine into our glasses. We drank, We laughed, We kissed, We looked at the stars. It was a night id never forget. We started to kiss again... We ended up going back to her room then the night entailed romance and love. I received love, I gave love. We fell asleep, and in the middle of the night I woke up next to her. We had been laying together side by side, I was holding her. I got up to take a piss and ran to her backdoor which was connected to the laundry room I couldn't make it, then... I pissed myself. She had woke up and opened the door the lights were off she said "Is everything okay?" I replied "I pissed myself" "Give me your jeans" She threw my jeans in a washer and said "Ill wash them in the morning babe" right there.. I knew the feeling I had was right. That she was the one Id be falling in love with... We went back to sleep. I woke up that morning hearing the washer and Sarah not in the bed. I was laying there smiling... She opened the door and said "My roommates are gone, We have the place to ourselves, Cereal?" I went to the kitchen with her to eat... We were standing and eating looking and smiling at eachother, and she started to say "I have school today but you can stay here..." and she then explained how she would ride her skateboard to the closest bus stop and then to the metro center to take another bus to the university. I told her "Ill go with you". She gave me my jeans and we headed to the bus stop. We walked there, Talking about stuff and looked each other in the eyes deeply... it was almost so unreal but so real for me. We got on the bus and rode to the metro. Then we waited for the next bus, The bus to the university arrived and she said we can meet her at this time.. I told her of course. We kissed and she went to school that day...

AROUND TOWN
LOST BOY

I rode around that day, Looking for food. I found a pizzeria, and told the owner about my travels. He told me, You come here at this time every other day I'll give you a slice of pizza. Then I got two slices that day for free, ate them and kept doing my workouts... the day went on to later, I had just explored. Then I noticed it was time to meet Sarah back at the bus stop... I got there and waited. The bus arrived and she came out holding her skateboard with a big smile... We kissed and headed back to her place. She asked me what I did all day, and I told her I worked out and did 100 pushups haha. We got to her place and just chilled really. We were laying on her bed and she was showing me pics of her, and music she had liked. We listened to music and talked all night... We kissed, We laughed, We loved... then we turned off the light..

The next morning we woke up and she had brought me some cereal in bed.. We were eating and laughing and then we smoked some joints. She had explained she didn't have work or school that day. So we relaxed, She washed all my clothes. We shared some stories and we talked about things we wanted in life. It was so different because their interests were so alike. We wanted the same things, a family, an adventure, a successful career. Something. We both wanted to start a clothing brand, We both wanted to live in a van or a RV, We wanted to have children. That day we drew logo ideas and drew whatever we talked about, We kissed, We laughed, We Loved...

The next few days, We spent together she introduced me to her roommates she had gone to college with. I would walk her to the bus stop every morning and every afternoon I would wait for her to come home. There were days I'd walk her to work, there were days we spent at the beach. There were days we hung at the arcade, We made are togetherness one. We made love, We connected. She was a real dealbreaker for me. I would be doing anything for her. One week I got a little sick and she took care of me and got me right before I got sick bad. It was a mild cold but she got me cold medicine and vitamin packets. We laid together at nights and we stared deeply into each other's eyes.

You didn't have to run and Hide.

One day around the time I had been feeling better, we were talking one morning and she explained she had been dealing with a past addiction. A addiction to heroine. I almost broke down. I didnt I tried to stay strong as possible, later that day she had brought up a topic I didn't think she would but it was meth. She asked me if I had ever tried it, I told her I was an addict for awhile but I had been sober for quite sometime since I met her. She then she asked me if I could get some. I told her no. She seemed upset. I told her, if she was planning on doing and to do it with me and not to do it out and around. That was my shit response... A few days went back and forth with the loss of a connection.. I was still falling in love with her. She started coming home late, nights seem to get a bit more stranger. One night she had came back and wanted to go right to sleep which she had never done, I laid there all night as she fell asleep. I was looking at her for a few hours wondering what I did wrong. Then all of a sudden. She started trembling, She started shaking, she basically and convulsing... as she was sleeping, I was scared. I didn't know what to do, but I did what I did. I held her up, and rocked her back a fourth slowly, I didn't know what was happening... She ended up calming down... and we fell back asleep... we woke up, I told her. I was angry with her, and asked her if she got high last night. She told me no. That day I walked her to the bus stop and I rode my skateboard all around town... looking for something. For some dope, not Mary jane. I found some, a tiny bit.. and returned to the bus stop around the time she got back from school. We walked home. And we were just so disconnected. We got back to her place and I told her I got some dope. She was somewhat happy, and you could probably understand what happened next. Yes we got high, and I had relapsed after being straight solid line for 5 months. We didn't smoke it, We didn't inject it, We snorted it like cocaine. It wasn't a lot. And yes we got high. I don't want to go into the high, but we ended up sleeping that night. The dope might have no have been that strong or something. But the next day, was the first day we argued. She had been talking about how she was going to spend her money that her parents gave her on some more dope. Not heroine, I told her no. I told her not again. The day went on, I can't even remember what I did throughout that day, I had just been waiting for her because I didn't know what was about to happen. I waited at the bus stop, and she didn't show up. So I went to hang out Gabriel I told him what was going on, he basically told me to try and stay away. Just as we started to hang, I looked to the left and there was Sarah riding by.... With some I could only guess were druggies. There my love was going to get high... I rode my skateboard back to her place and sat in the front until she came home... it went from about 2 to 8/9 at night. She rode up to me and saw me laying in front of the house and said "What are you doing?" I already knew something was wrong. We argued... then she invited me back inside and we kissed, and made love once more.. the connection was rough. The next morning we were both pretty quiet and we headed to the bus so she could get to class. We waited for the bus, at this moment. I wasn't about to put myself through this, and get hurt. The bus showed up she got up to give me a hug, then she gave me a kiss. I knew I wouldn't be back to wait for her again... I rode up all the way to the North end of Santa Cruz and put my thumb out, I was getting OUT. I refused to relapse completely and to keep getting high on dope with someone I had just fell completely in love with. It only was about 10 mins, a silver four door showed up and a young guy rolled down the window and said how far? "As far as we can go"

There I ran away from my baby girl. My love

15

WHERE THE GRASS IS GREENER

I rode so far away… I was still on my way to Mt.Shasta. I had ended up riding with the guy all the way to San Francisco his car broke down and I helped him find someone to help him repair it. In return he offered a ride all the way North. We rode. I arrived in Arcata California, It was colorful, and so peaceful. This place I had never been, I hung out here and there. On the plaza, around the redwoods, I went back to doing my workouts, I started sunbathing more. Then one day I was walking to grocery store to get oatmeal and there were these people smoking in a green suburban. I heard "Hey, You want to smoke?" It was a little bit of a older guy with a hat and some skater clothes on. He introduced himself, His name was Hans, this guy would end up being one of my bestest of friends later on. We smoked and he showed me around Arcata a bit more. I told him I slept behind the library and then the next day he woke up…. Talking about a show in eureka, and invited me. He said he buy the ticket, We ended up hanging for a few days before the show, then headed to eureka to see this show. The Rosewater cover band for The Grateful Dead. It was on someone's property, someone's backyard, with redwoods. We set up, And I started asking him for mushrooms, he said he didn't want to give them to me because he thought I wouldnt be responsible. Then we all kind of separated and the show had started the night had begun and people started tripping. Left and right people were just HIGH, on what… idk. So I sat down and started to listen to the music. I looked to my left and there was this guy *with long curly hair and sunglasses on, we started chatting. Even though the music was loud we were talking about acid and mushrooms. He told me that he didn't have mushrooms, but he cold hook me up me some acid. I said f*** it. We walked up and a little bit away from the stage and to a tent. There was a group of oldies with long curly hair and they all had sunglasses on in the middle of the night, the guy I had met told another guy "This is the kid" the dude opened his purple jacket and reached for a big square sheet, black and purple. He took one tab and handed it to me, "Take it right here".. I said thank you. I said f*** it. I put it on my tongue and walked off. I walked back to the stage and stood there, not even 5 mins later I seen Hans. He was waving at me to come over to him on the side of the stage. I went over to him and he said "Ready?" He pointed down and showed me a double ziplock baggie full of mushrooms. He opened the bag, and we both bear clawed to basically the bottom of the bag. I had walked off, And yes started tripping. I went through me trip, it was long and very strange. Yes, I enjoyed what I could of the show. I ended up having to be babysitted by Hans back in the suburban because I was so high. It wasn't over yet, even in the morning…. We headed back to Arcata, and I had a whole new HIGH! MUSHYS !!! So I started to get very, VERY high on them. At this point, I wasn't thinking of Sarah. I was getting HIGH. Then I remember one day Hans, offered to take me to Mt.Shasta, Because I told him I really was trying to get there… So we went. Hans, Gio, Latill, Niko, and Me. We drove all the way to Panther Meadows to the top of the mountain bought our 2 days on the mountain and set up camp. As we were setting up, It started to blizzard. Then we all huddled up by a fire as the snow settled down. Gio and Latills friends had met us there and they had mushrooms as well, so did Niko and so did Hans. Everyone made a decision to cook up some mushroom stew. They did. We had two little pots, a blue one, and a black one, and they went around in the circle. We all had our share. Then the snow started and Gabriel, Gios friend asked me "You ever play a Mandolin?" I replied " I haven't" He handed it over to me and I started to play this Mandolin on the mountain next to the fire. On the mountain. It sounded good, there was a mystic in the air. The next few days I was really, really high. We drove from Mt.Shasta to Ashland*

Oregon to a bathhouse, we all got right within or spirit with the water there. Then we turned around back to Arcata. It was along 7/8 days. I was eating mushrooms, Tripping. Hallucinating. We got back to Arcata and I had got into a argument with Hans and we separated. I ended up eating more mushrooms, went down the 101 and had a adventure I will, never forget. I ended up realizing, I left my love. I left her helpless, and high. I felt terrible. I tried getting back to her, I was very far away from Santa cruz... it didn't work. I ended up in a Psych ward..... twice... It wasn't good... they decided to move me back to arizona... the sedated me, hired a private security firm to escort me to the airport and flew me to Arizona.... To home...

WHERE ARE YOU?

When I got home, I spent a few weeks at a psych hospital in arizona. When I got out, I reconnected with a few friends there. First thing was first, get a hold of my girl..... I did. I found her contact through a friend that I had contacted when I was with her... I got a hold of her. We talked on the phone, She told me she was home in LA living with her parents again.. We talked every other day. Every other night... I told her I loved her, She said she loved me. Then the one chance I had, My dad invited me to California for Christmas. I told her I was going to see her. She said okay. I headed to California, I spent time with my family and waited for Christmas. My dad gave me $100 for Christmas and I already knew what I wanted to do. I wanted to see my baby. So I asked my big brother to take me to Northridge to see my girl... he said sure. Then my little brother said he wanted to come... I called her. And she said come pick me up. We all got in the car, and headed up Northridge. It was about two hours from Costa mesa. We got there at the gas station and she told me she was crossing the street.... I jumped out of the car and ran straight to her... She jumped right into my arms. I was holding her by her legs and kissing her. We got in the car, and decided to go to Venice to spend the day together. We drove there, as we did. I sat in the back with her, with our seat belts off... We kissed and *held each other.... I told her face to face. I would marry her one day. We got to Venice beach, Walked to the handball court for my big brother, as big brother played Sarah Me and my little brother sat on the side talking... the first time I started taking medication my legs would tremble and shake alot.. She saw that.. and touched my leg and the instantaneously stopped shaking. She said let's smoke? She loaded a bowl, and us three started to walk to the sand... We sat near the water and started smoking... Even my little brother hit it.... Ahahaha.. What a time. The last time I saw her face to face.. We walked back to the hand ball court and I bought her some pizza. She ate, as she did my big brother started to tell me that we couldn't take her back home. I was furious, I couldn't show it though. Due to me being on meds and just visiting, I was basically suppose to just head back with my brothers, I had to explain to her about how we had to leave. How I had to leave her.... If I knew this I would have done it way differently... We walked to the car and I gripped her tight, I kissed her. And told her I loved her, Even though I knew she probably thought not. Thought I was a piece of shit after that. Idk, but it would have been the last time I seen her since this day... She walked off and my brothers and I got into the car. We drove off and as we did I seen my baby girl once again.. walking to the bus stop. And there and then I could see it in her face she was hurt, I didn't know how to react. It was all happening way to fast..*

<u>*And it left such deep wound...*</u>

the bus stop on windward..

SARAH SMILE

It wasn't the last time I talked to her... but the last time I talked to her would be the last time we talked... We never had closure. We never ended, we always were something. The drugs were in the way, and the addiction was painful. Not just for me, for her. Some people are strong, some people are weak. I don't wish I would have done things differently if the day arised and I was back with her in her room in Santa Cruz. I would have been a strict boyfriend. I would have not been weak, I would have been right. We all make mistakes, and it's very unfortunate that the girl I fell deeply oh so deeply in love with was the one I made one of the biggest mistakes with. I still search the web for her, I still think about her. I still think about us..

Recently I thought I had the right information to contact her. Turns out it's not what I thought, It's the worst. It's been years, Years since I met her. And she is out there. Not doing good. If this ever reaches where I'd like it to, And it gets to her. <u>Sarah, I love you. Please. Please get better, Be stronger, and stop using. Please love</u>

To my twin flame

Yes this is a true story......

I wrote this February 26th 2024 at 12 AM, and stayed up until 5 AM writing....

This is my first book….

The picture that says "<u>The Incredible True Story</u>" is a mural right infront of where we met…..Before it was different *and Thank you…… To all that read it*

Honey, I cried, too
You better believe it
Honey, my heart still beats for you
Even though you don't feel it
Honey, I cried, too
You better believe it
Honey, my heart still beats for you
Even though you don't feel it beating

MAC DEMARCO